THE LEGEND OF GOLD

for children 8 to 12 years

Music by Pattie France   Words by Dixie Atkins

Edited by Alison Hedger

A story with music and choral speaking. Suitable for use as a dramatic mini-musical including mime, costume and dance, or as a concert performance. The work is also useful as an integral part of the curriculum.

1. Indian Lullaby
2. Squaw Horse
3. Dance of the Totem
4. Hunting Song
5. The Fight
6. The Prayer of Golden Arrow
7. Story-teller

Each song has a piano accompaniment with unison vocal line and optional guitar chords. There is a cue at the start of each song to assist the pianist.

Parts for recorder and unpitched percussion are also included – these instruments are suggestions. Any appropriate melodic and percussive instruments can be used.

Golden Apple Productions
Beckley
Hinton
Christchurch
Dorset BH23 7EB

Telephone: 0425 617106

© Golden Apple Productions 1987 – 'The Legend of Golden Arrow'
First published in U.K. 1988 by Golden Apple Productions.
Publication © Golden Apple Productions 1988

ISBN 1 870997 04 2

The starting point for this topic was a visit to America. I described my trip to the children and told them about an Indian reservation that I had seen. Such was the interest of my Junior class that we chose North American Indians as our topic for the term.

We began with a flow chart and from this each group chose a topic; clothes, food, customs, war, work, the modern Indian. Each group was named after an Indian tribe, and each child invented an Indian name for his/her self.

The topic was cross-curricula. The children made their own books, containing both fact and fiction. These were read to the class. They used 'wampum' beads as currency in Maths. They made Indian head-dresses and masks; constructed an Indian village; carved a totem pole; made bead patterns; painted sign language pictures. We even had an unsuccessful attempt at smoke signals! But no scalping, despite requests from the boys!

In Drama the children improvised war dances and hunting and acted out Custer's Last Stand, and the tale of Hiawatha. Noisy but enjoyable!

As the fourth year Juniors always gave an end-of-term concert, which was my responsibility, it seemed logical to pursue the Indian theme. I wrote the story and the words of the songs, then asked Mrs. France, our music teacher, to write the music. The concert was a great success, enjoyed by children and parents. It was a very satisfactory climax to our topic.

Dixie Atkins

Tempo and stylistic instructions are given, but I have not added any dynamics. I think that these are best governed by the words and the feelings of the performers.

Pattie France

© Golden Apple Productions 1988 – 'The Legend of Golden Arrow'

Books Used For My Own Class Project

Hopi Rain Dance	Cambridge University Press
Tales of the North American Indians	Hodder & Stoughton
The Plains Indians	Macdonald
Indians of the North American Plains	Macdonald
North American Indians	Macdonald
The American West	Wayland
North American Indians	Wayland
Buffaloes	Wayland
The Plains Indians	Oliver & Boyd
The Story of the Indians	Ladybird
Custer's Last Stand	Ladybird
North American Mammals	Ladybird

I also used the poem of 'Hiawatha' by Longfellow, and a superb book of photographs – Portraits of North American Indian Life by Edward Curtis published by Promontory Publication Incorporated.

Dixie Atkins

**The texts for choral speaking are in heavier type.
It may be preferred to give these parts to individuals.**

© Golden Apple Productions 1988 – 'The Legend of Golden Arrow'

THE LEGEND OF GOLDEN ARROW

**The night is in retreat,
Defeated by the dawn.
And as the shadows die
An Indian child is born.**

Long ago, in the land of America, there lived a mighty tribe of Red Indians, known as the Sioux. They were fierce warriors and skilful hunters, and their chief was the greatest of all.

One starless night, a baby was born in the teepee of the chief. His father was filled with joy and pride.

'This is my son. He shall be a great warrior and all men shall fear him. He shall be a mighty chief and all men shall know his name. He shall be called Golden Arrow.'

The mother smiled. Cradling her baby in her arms, she sang softly to her child.

SONG   1. Indian Lullaby

1. When the night wind sighs,
     when the night bird flies,
   Indian baby, lullaby.
   When the grey wolf howls,
     when the brown bear prowls,
   Indian baby, mother's by.

Chorus   Sleep, my little Golden Arrow.
           I will keep you safe and warm.
         Sleep, my tiny Indian warrior.
           I will guard you from the storm.

2. When the shadows creep,
     when the camp-fires sleep,
   Indian baby, hush your cries.
   When the cold moon shines,
     when the pye-dog whines,
   Indian baby, close your eyes.

Chorus   Sleep, my little Golden Arrow . . .

3. When the world is dumb,
     when the spirits come,
   Indian baby, have no fear.
   Soon the dawn will break,
     soon all creatures wake,
   Indian baby, day is here.

Chorus   Sleep, my little Golden Arrow . . .

**Dusty, dirty, Indian baby,
Crawling on the hard baked ground;
Picking blades of sun-parched grasses;
Counting pebbles, smooth and round.**

© Golden Apple Productions 1988 – 'The Legend of Golden Arrow'

As Golden Arrow grew older, he loved to ride on his mother's back, safely held in a brightly coloured blanket. He twisted his tiny hands into the long plaits of her hair, as he swung and bumped behind her.

SONG 2. Squaw Horse

1. Prancing horse with flaring nostrils
   Very fine for warrior tall.
   Papoose needs a steed less fiery.
   Squaw horse is the best of all.

Chorus Squaw horse. Squaw horse.
   I'm as proud as a chief.
   Squaw horse. Squaw horse.
   The bright sky above and my squaw horse beneath.

2. Through the bustling tent encampment
   Squaw horse trots with head held high.
   From my swaying blanket saddle
   I can watch the world go by.

Chorus Squaw horse . . .

3. There's the chief, now old in wisdom,
   Dreaming of the battles won.
   There's old grandma, gnarled and toothless,
   Squatting silent in the sun.

Chorus Squaw horse . . .

4. There are squaws, bedecked with wampum,
   There, the totem, strange and tall.
   There, a brave with feathered head-dress.
   Totem watches over all.

Chorus Squaw horse . . .

5. There are fires, and there are teepees,
   There are children, berry-brown,
   Laughing, calling, fighting, squalling.
   Mother! Mother! Set me down!

Chorus Squaw horse . . .

**My bow is made of maple,
My arrows swiftly fly.
My aim is sure and steady,
My arrows touch the sky.**

Soon, Golden Arrow left his mother's side and wandered around the camp on his own sturdy legs. One day his father handed him a small bow and some feathered arrows.

'Soon you will be a man, my son. Practise every day. When you can bend the bow and shoot the arrows straight and true, you shall join the hunt.'

© Golden Apple Productions 1988 – 'The Legend of Golden Arrow'

In his excitement, the little boy shot his arrows wildly, so his play-mates shouted and scattered. He ran to his mother.

'Look, Mother, I am a great hunter'

His mother smiled and turned away.

That night, Golden Arrow was too excited to sleep. He watched the braves, as they danced wildly around the Totem.

'One day, I, too, shall take my place with the warriors, and dance in the firelight.'

SONG

3. Dance of the Totem

1. Hear the beat, steady beat of the rhythm.
   Through the night steals the soft pulsing sound.
   See the braves, solemn-faced, take their places.
   Hear their feet padding slow on the ground.

Chorus Totem dance, totem dance, totem dance.
   Totem dance, totem dance, totem dance.

2. Round the pole, totem pole, move the dancers.
   Dust flies up from their bare flying feet.
   Shadows crouched in the swift-stealing twilight
   Silent sway to the fast rising beat.

Chorus Totem dance . . .

3. Whirling forms, swirling forms, twisting, twirling,
   Swiftly turn in the flickering light;
   Wildly weaving a crazy crescendo,
   Cutting patterns of fear through the night.

Chorus Totem dance . . .

**See the fingers of the dawn light,
Creeping, stealthy, through the camp;
Drawing back the night-time shadows;
Lighting day-time's glorious lamp.**

One morning, his father came to where Golden Arrow slept.

'Wake up, little one. Today we hunt.'

Golden Arrow was very sleepy but he obeyed his father. Taking his bow and arrows, he crept from the teepee. His mother watched him go.

Outside the hunters waited. Golden Arrow was lifted onto his father's horse. At first, he was afraid. The ground seemed so far away. But his father's strong arms gave him courage.

They galloped swiftly across the plains. Soon the buffalo were sighted and the hunt began.

© Golden Apple Productions 1988 – 'The Legend of Golden Arrow'

SONG   4. Hunting Song

Buffalo and bear – Beware!
The hunters are about – Look out!

1. On stealthy feet the hunters creep,
   And where the purple shadows sleep,
   They stalk in solemn silence deep.
   Alone.

Buffalo and bear – Take care!
Now lift your head and hear – They're near!

2. From taut-strung bows the arrows bright
   Soar, in a multi-coloured flight.
   And nostrils flare in sudden fright.
   Alone.

Buffalo and bear – Despair!
But still in fear you wait – Too late!

3. And homeward now in tired content,
   His back beneath the burden bent,
   Each hunter turns towards his tent.
   Alone.

Welcome, hunters of the Sioux!
Welcome, raiders of the plain!
Welcome, warriors brave and true!
Welcome to our camp again!

The braves returned laden with the bodies of the buffaloes. The warriors were happy and sang as they strode through the camp. But Golden Arrow ran to his mother, and there were tears in his eyes.

'The buffalo were so beautiful – and we killed them.'

'It was necessary, my son. We need their meat for food; their skins to make clothing and teepees.'

'I hate killing. I do not want to be a warrior or a hunter.'

'Then you must find another way.'

'What shall I do?'

'Wait, my son. Age will bring wisdom.'

But when Golden Arrow told the other boys of his feelings, they laughed at him and called him a coward. And so he fought.

© *Golden Apple Productions 1988 – 'The Legend of Golden Arrow'*

SONG

5. The Fight

1. Through the camp the boys are calling –
      'Come and see the fight!'
   Big ones running, small ones crawling –
      Come and see the fight!
   Now the two opponents meet,
   Lashing hands and whirling feet.
   Meet and part.
   Pounding heart.
   Who will win the fight?

2. Little Hawk and Golden Arrow –
      Come and see the fight!
   Hemmed within a circle narrow –
      Come and see the fight!
   Gleaming bodies caked with dust.
   Swift retreat and sudden thrust.
   Will it be
   Victory?
   Who will win the fight?

3. Mouths a-gape with expectation –
      Come and see the fight!
   Eyes a-glow – anticipation –
      Come and see the fight!
   Hawk has fallen. Arrow too.
   Now the fight begins anew.
   Crowd is dumb.
   Now a hum.
   Who will win the fight?

4. Hear, a mighty roar is swelling –
      Come and see the fight!
   From a score of throats it's welling –
      Come and see the fight!
   Little Hawk is on the ground.
   Golden Arrow dances round.
   Fight is done.
   Who has won?
   Golden Arrow! Hey!

Girls dance. Boys fight.
Horses prance. Boys fight.
Babies scream. Boys fight.
Old men dream but boys fight.

Although Golden Arrow won the fight, his father was disappointed in him.

'You cannot live in the tribe, if you do not take your share of the work. It is a man's task to hunt.'

Then the mother spoke.

'Leave him, my husband. He is but a boy. When he is a man, the decision will be made.'

In the Sioux tribe, a boy became a man at fifteen. The night before his fifteenth birthday, Golden Arrow left the camp and rode out to the plains. There he prayed to the Great Spirit.

© *Golden Apple Productions 1988 – 'The Legend of Golden Arrow'*

SONG

6. The Prayer of Golden Arrow

1. Spirit that guides and guards and comforts,
   Come to your son tonight.
   Here on this lonely silent hillside,
   Bathe me in gentle light.

Chorus   Spirit, Great Spirit of love and joy,
Hear the prayer of an Indian boy.

2. There, far below, the fires are burning;
   There, where my tribe now sleep.
   Here, on the hill, the night wind whispers,
   Softly the shadows creep.

Chorus   Spirit, Great Spirit . . .

3. I have been named a loathsome coward.
   I have no wish to kill.
   Look in my heart and treat me justly.
   Tell all my fears, 'Be still!'

Chorus   Spirit, Great Spirit . . .

4. You, who know all and love your children,
   Soothe away every fear.
   Give me the gift to speak in beauty,
   That all the tribe may hear.

Chorus   Spirit, Great Spirit . . .

**Although I am alone,
I do not fear the night.
For far upon the hills
I see a wondrous light.**

Golden Arrow seemed to hear a quiet voice.

'Each one has his part to play. You have a gentle heart. You cannot kill. There are many mighty warriors in the tribe of the Sioux. These braves do great deeds. You shall be their recorder. Gather together all the legends of your tribe. Tell them and retell them, so that none will ever forget their past. Teach the children, so that they, in turn, may teach their children. Go now, and take your part.'

**Noisy children, leave your playing.
Busy mothers, gather near.
Listen to the story-teller,
Weaving tales of joy and fear.**

© Golden Apple Productions 1988 – 'The Legend of Golden Arrow'

Golden Arrow became a great Shaman, which means, story-teller, and was loved and respected by all his tribe. His name was changed from GOLDEN ARROW to GOLDEN TONGUE.

SONG   7. Story-teller

1. I will tell you a tale of the buffalo hunt.
   I will tell you a tale of the fight.
   I will speak to your heart in the beauty of words.
   I will speak to your heart in the night.

Chorus   Story-teller, Story-teller!
   Tell a story, Story-teller!

2. I will weave you a dream of the eagle that soars.
   I will weave you a dream of desire.
   I will sing you a song that will win your applause.
   I will sing you a song of the fire.

Chorus   Story-teller . . .

3. I will speak you a legend that tells of the Sioux.
   I will speak you a legend of pain.
   I will rhyme you a rhyme of the land and the sky.
   I will rhyme you a rhyme of the plain.

Chorus   Story-teller . . .

4. I'm a weaver of dreams; I'm a singer of songs;
   I'm a teller of tales, short and long.
   For my name is renowned in the tribe of the Sioux.
   GOLDEN ARROW is now GOLDEN TONGUE.

THE END

© Golden Apple Productions 1988 – 'The Legend of Golden Arrow'

© Golden Apple Productions 1988 – 'The Legend of Golden Arrow'

1.
Indian Lullaby

Cue: The mother smiled. Cradling her baby in her arms, she sang softly to her child.

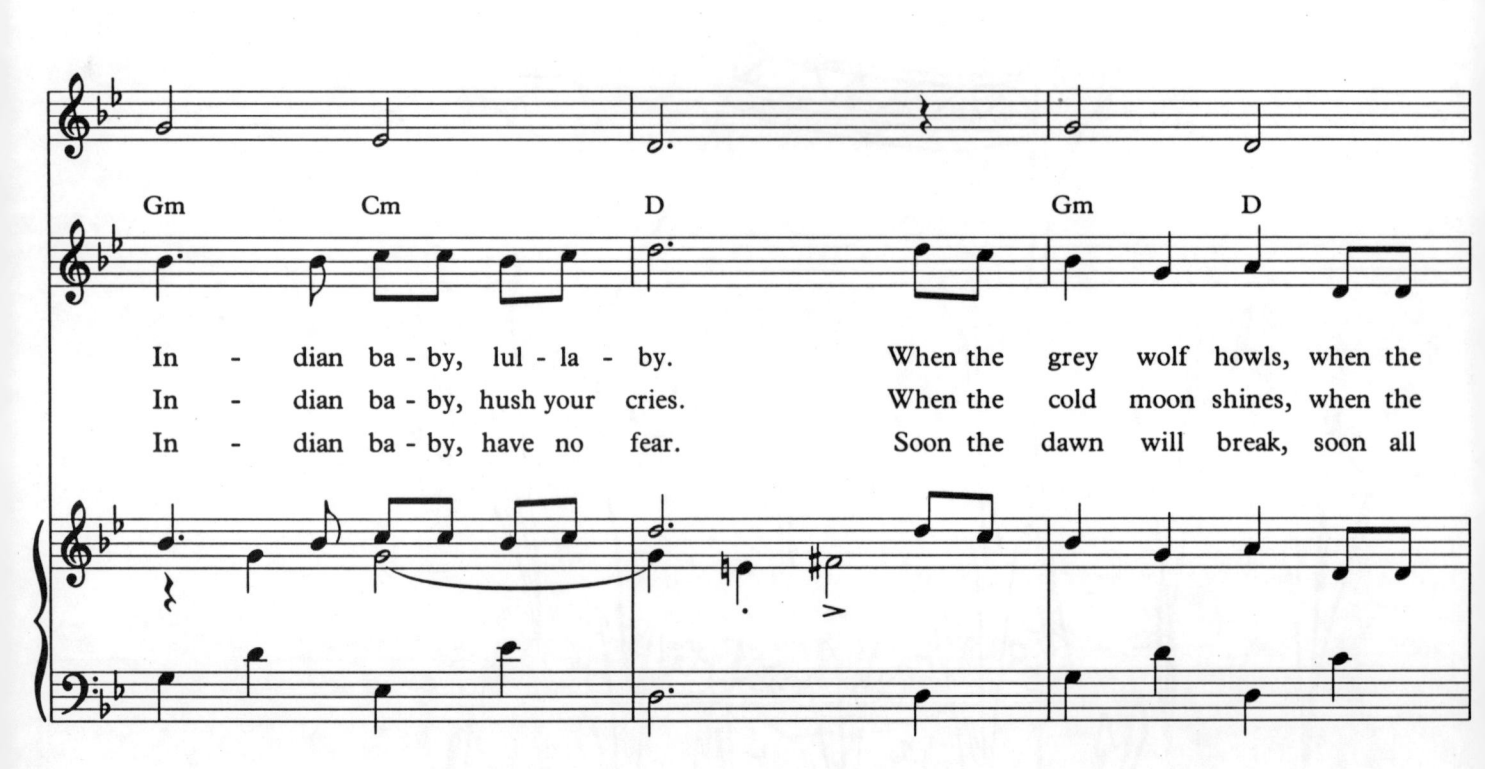

RECORDER

♩ = 104

Gently and Smoothly

1. When the night wind sighs, when the night bird flies,
2. When the sha-dows creep, when the camp-fires sleep,
3. When the world is dumb, when the spi-rits come,

In - dian ba - by, lul - la - by. When the grey wolf howls, when the
In - dian ba - by, hush your cries. When the cold moon shines, when the
In - dian ba - by, have no fear. Soon the dawn will break, soon all

© Golden Apple Productions 1988 – 'The Legend of Golden Arrow'

Gm		Cm	D7 · G

brown bear prowls, In-dian ba-by, mo-ther's by.
pye-dog whines, In-dian ba-by, close your eyes.
crea-tures wake, In-dian ba-by, day is here.

RECORDER

XYLOPHONE
G · C · D7 · Bm

Sleep, my lit-tle Gol-den Ar-row. I will keep you safe and warm.

CHORUS

Em · Am · G · D7 · G

Sleep, my ti-ny In-dian war-rior. I will guard you from the storm.

© Golden Apple Productions 1988 – 'The Legend of Golden Arrow'

2.
Squaw Horse

Cue: He twisted his tiny hands into the long plaits of her hair, as he swung and bumped behind her.

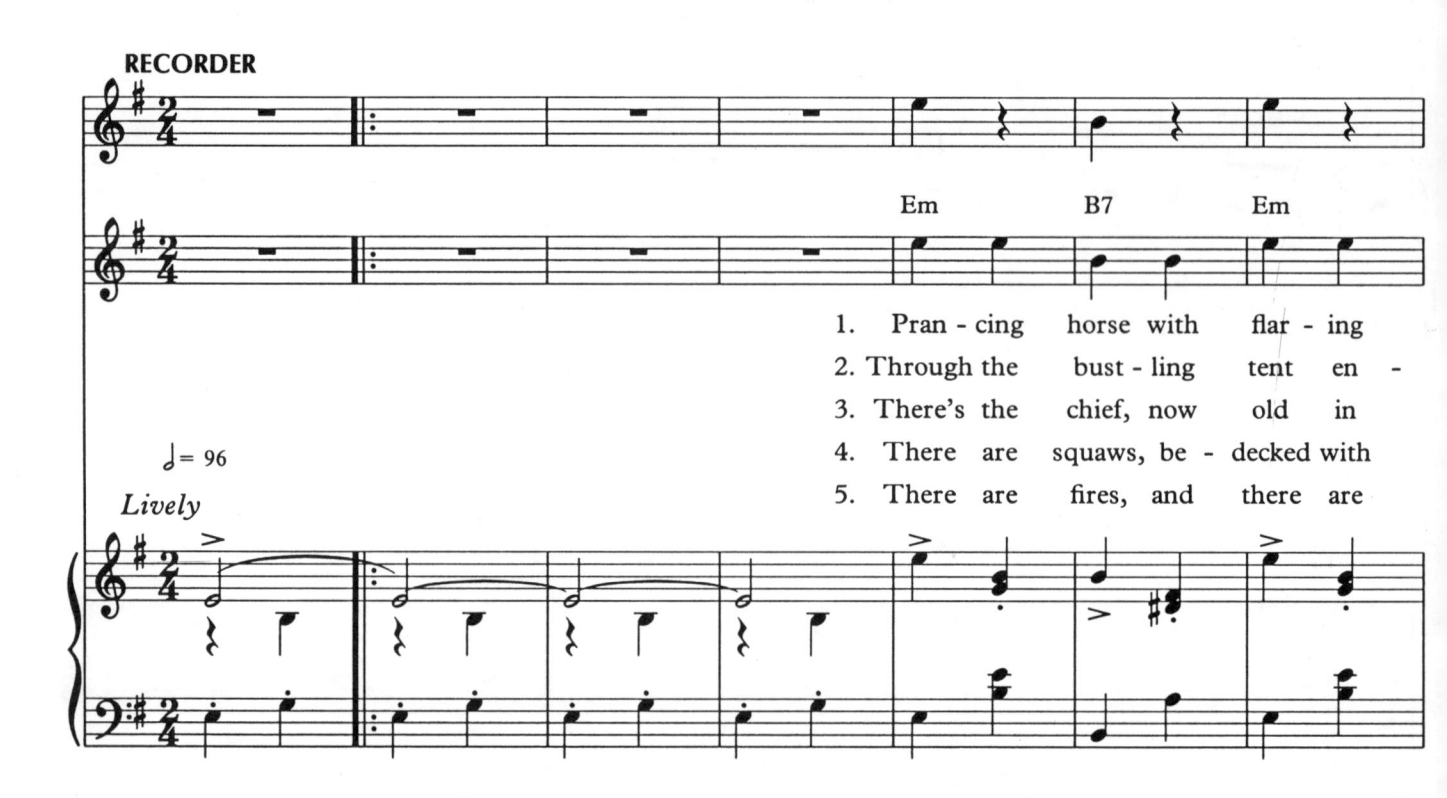

RECORDER

♩ = 96
Lively

1. Pran - cing horse with flar - ing nos - trils Ve - ry fine for wa - rrior tall. Pa - poose
2. Through the bust - ling tent en - camp - ment Squaw horse trots with head held high. From my
3. There's the chief, now old in wis - dom, Dream - ing of the bat - tles won. There's old
4. There are squaws, be - decked with wam - pum, There, the to - tem, strange and tall. There, a
5. There are fires, and there are tee - pees, There are chil - dren, ber - ry - brown, Laugh - ing,

Tambourine ‖: 2/4 ♩ 𝄽 :‖

© Golden Apple Productions 1988 – 'The Legend of Golden Arrow'

needs a steed less fie-ry. Squaw horse is the best of all.
sway-ing blan-ket sad-dle I can watch the world go by.
grand-ma, gnarled and tooth-less, Squat-ting si-lent in the sun.
brave with fea-thered head-dress. To-tem wat-ches ov-er all.
call-ing, fight-ing, squall-ing. Mo-ther! Mo-ther! Set me down!

CHORUS
Squaw horse. Squaw horse. I'm as proud as a chief. Squaw horse.

Squaw horse. The bright sky a-bove and my squaw horse be-neath.

© *Golden Apple Productions* 1988 – 'The Legend of Golden Arrow'

3.
Totem Dance

Cue: 'One day, I, too, shall take my place with the warriors, and dance in the firelight.'

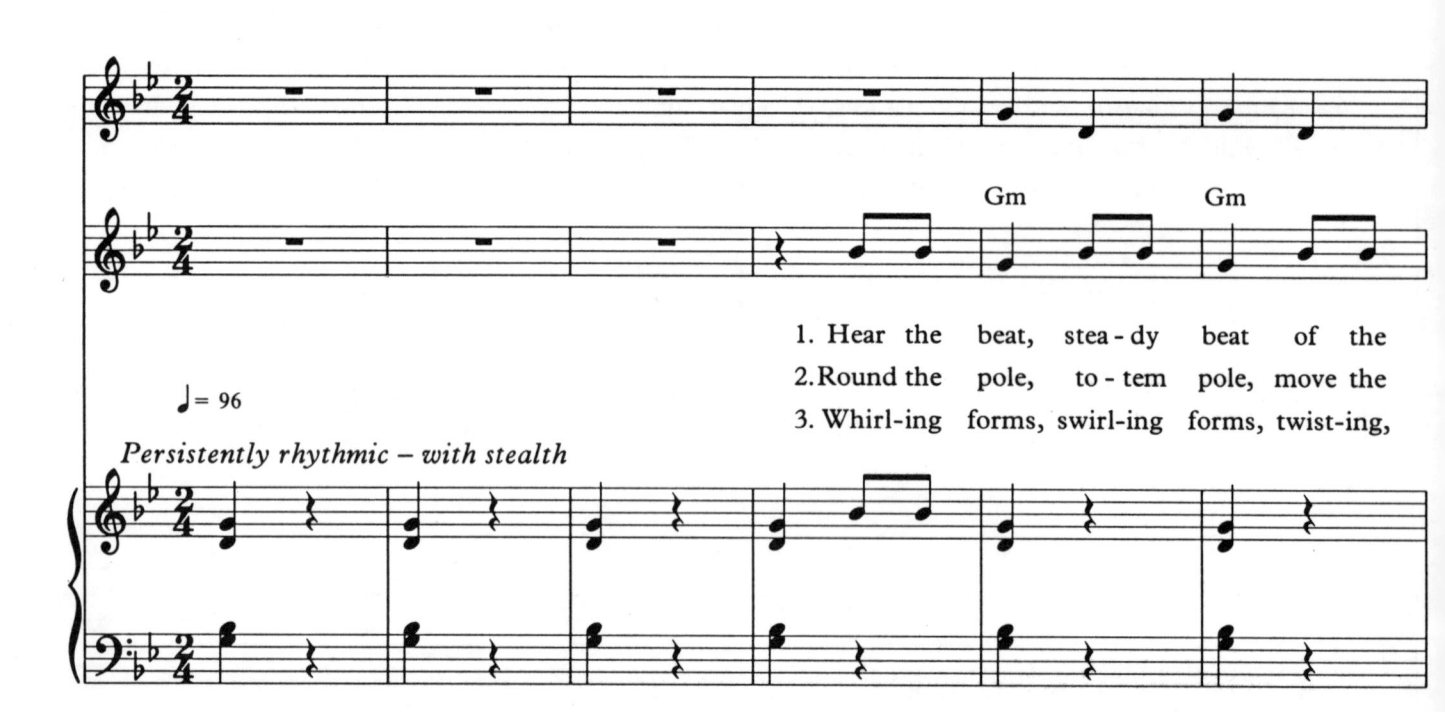

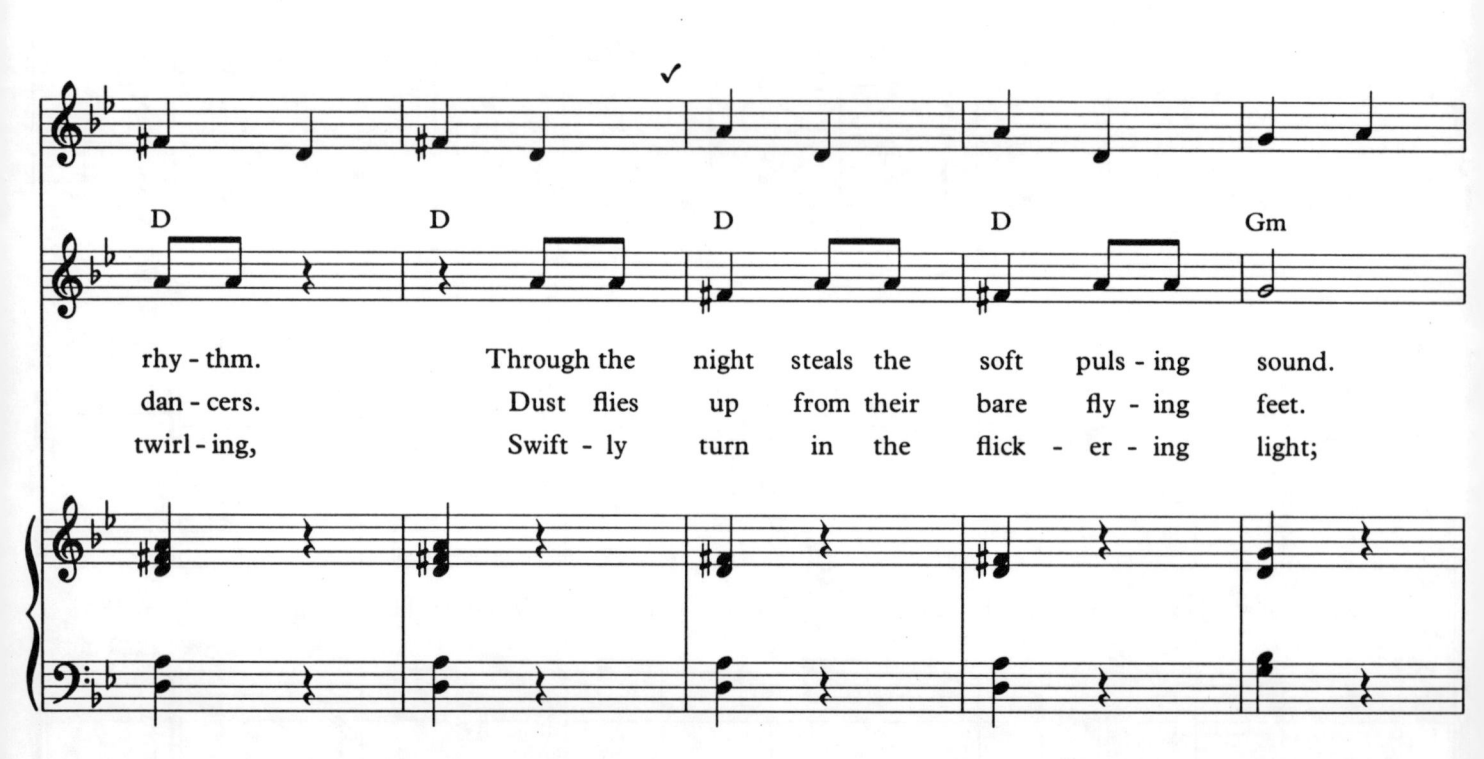

Persistently rhythmic – with stealth
♩ = 96

1. Hear the beat, stea-dy beat of the rhy-thm. Through the night steals the soft puls-ing sound.
2. Round the pole, to-tem pole, move the dan-cers. Dust flies up from their bare fly-ing feet.
3. Whirl-ing forms, swirl-ing forms, twist-ing, twirl-ing, Swift-ly turn in the flick-er-ing light;

© Golden Apple Productions 1988 – 'The Legend of Golden Arrow'

See the braves, solemn-faced, take their places. Hear their feet padding slow on the ground.
Shadows crouched in the swift-stealing twilight Silent sway to the fast rising beat.
Wildly weaving a crazy crescendo, Cutting patterns of fear through the night.

CHORUS
Totem dance, totem dance, totem dance. Totem dance, totem dance, totem dance.

© Golden Apple Productions 1988 – 'The Legend of Golden Arrow'

4.
Hunting Song

Cue: Soon the buffalo were sighted and the hunt began.

Mysteriously

Introduction only

BUFFALO AND BEAR – BEWARE!
THE HUNTERS ARE ABOUT – LOOK OUT!

BUFFALO AND BEAR – TAKE CARE!
NOW LIFT YOUR HEAD AND HEAR – THEY'RE NEAR!

BUFFALO AND BEAR – DESPAIR!
BUT STILL IN FEAR YOU WAIT – TOO LATE!

RECORDER

1. On steal-thy feet the hun-ters creep, And where the pur-ple sha-dows sleep, They
2. From taut-strung bows the ar-rows bright Soar, in a mul-ti-co-loured flight. And
3. And home-ward now in tired con-tent, His back be-neath the bur-den bent, Each

♩= 58

Mysteriously

© Golden Apple Productions 1988 – 'The Legend of Golden Arrow'

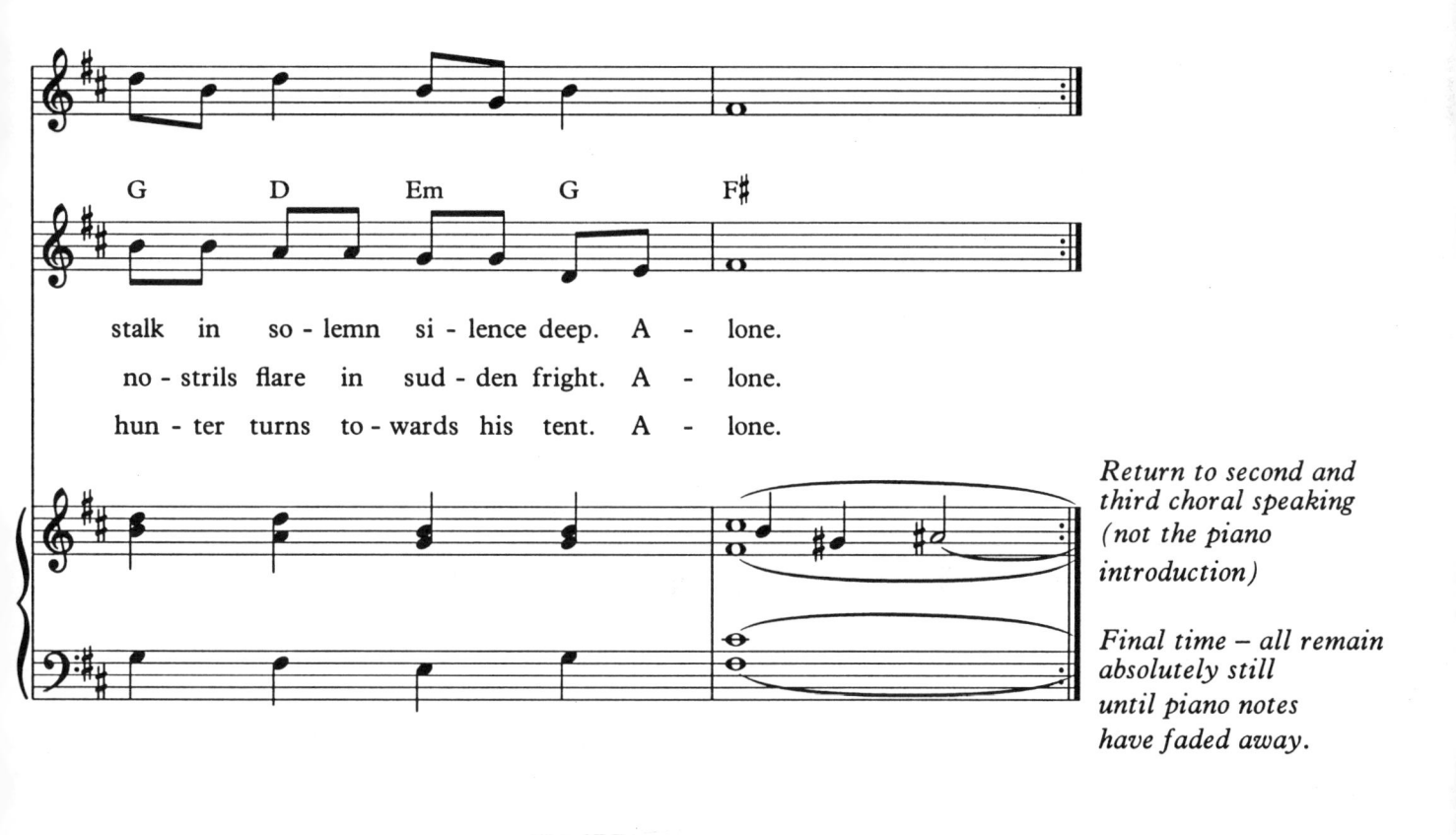

stalk in so-lemn si-lence deep. A-lone.
no-strils flare in sud-den fright. A-lone.
hun-ter turns to-wards his tent. A-lone.

Return to second and third choral speaking (not the piano introduction)

Final time – all remain absolutely still until piano notes have faded away.

© Golden Apple Productions 1988 – 'The Legend of Golden Arrow'

5.
The Fight

Cue: ...they laughed at him and called him a coward. And so he fought.

RECORDER

♩ = 120

A March

1. Through the camp the boys are call-ing
2. Lit - tle Hawk and Gol - den Ar - row
3. Mouths a - gape with ex - pec - ta - tion
4. Hear, a migh - ty roar is swell-ing

– 'Come and see the fight!' Big ones run-ning, small ones crawl-ing – Come and see the fight!
– Come and see the fight! Hemmed with-in a cir - cle nar-row – Come and see the fight!
– Come and see the fight! Eyes a - glow an - ti - ci - pa - tion – Come and see the fight!
– Come and see the fight! From a score of throats it's wel-ling – Come and see the fight!

© Golden Apple Productions 1988 – 'The Legend of Golden Arrow'

Now the two op-po-nents meet, Lash-ing hands and whirl-ing feet.
Gleam-ing bod-ies caked with dust. Swift re-treat and sud-den thrust.
Hawk has fal-len. Ar-row too. Now the fight be-gins a-new.
Lit-tle Hawk is on the ground. Gol-den Ar-row dan-ces round.

Meet and part. Pound-ing heart. Who will win the fight?
Will it be Vic-to-ry? Who will win the fight?
Crowd is dumb. Now a hum. Who will win the fight?
Fight is done. Who has won? Gol-den Ar-row! Hey!

Coconut shells – Wood Block

© Golden Apple Productions 1988 – 'The Legend of Golden Arrow'

6. The Prayer of Golden Arrow

Cue: ...out to the plains. There he prayed to the Great Spirit.

♩. = 48
Smoothly

1. Spi-rit that guides and guards and com-forts, Come to your son to - night._____ Here on this lone - ly
2. There, far be - low, the fires are burn - ing; There, where my tribe now sleep._____ Here, on the hill, the
3. I have been named a loath - some cow - ard. I have no wish to kill._____ Look in my heart and
4. You, who know all and love your chil - dren, Soothe a - way ev - ery fear._____ Give me the gift to

© Golden Apple Productions 1988 – 'The Legend of Golden Arrow'

si - lent hill - side, Bathe me in gen - tle light.
night wind whis - pers, Soft - ly the sha - dows creep.
treat me just - ly. Tell all my fears, 'Be still!'
speak in beau - ty, That all the tribe may hear.

Spi-rit, Great Spi-rit of love and joy, Hear the prayer of an In - di - an boy.

CHORUS

Drum ‖: 6/8 ♩. ♩. | ♩ ♪ ♩. :‖

© Golden Apple Productions 1988 – 'The Legend of Golden Arrow'

7.
Storyteller

Cue: His name was changed from GOLDEN ARROW to GOLDEN TONGUE.

RECORDER

♩. = 56
Gently and with feeling – Count 1 in a bar

F   C(G♯)   F   C   F   C   F

1. I will tell you a tale of the buf-fa-lo hunt._____
2. I will weave you a dream of the ea-gle that soars._____
3. I will speak you a le-gend that tells of the Sioux._____
4. I'm a wea-ver of dreams; I'm a sing-er of songs;_____

© Golden Apple Productions 1988 – 'The Legend of Golden Arrow'

C F C(G♯) F Am Dm Am Dm

I will tell you a tale of the fight.
I will weave you a dream of de-sire.
I will speak you a le-gend of pain.
I'm a tel-ler of tales, short and long.

Am Gm Gm E♭ E♭

I will speak to your heart in the beau-ty of words. I will
I will sing you a song that will win your ap-plause. I will
I will rhyme you a rhyme of the land and the sky. I will
For my name is re-nowned in the tribe of the Sioux. GOL-DEN

© Golden Apple Productions 1988 – 'The Legend of Golden Arrow'

speak to your heart in the night.
sing you a song of the fire. Sto - ry - tel - ler,
rhyme you a rhyme of the plain.
AR - ROW is now GOL - DEN TONGUE. **CHORUS**

Sto - ry - tel - ler! Tell a sto - ry, Sto - ry - tel - ler!

Final time only

© Golden Apple Productions 1988 – 'The Legend of Golden Arrow'